CW00523698

CORPS LEADER

Hints on leading a Salvation Army Corps

by

Bruce A Stevens

Copyright © 2016 by Bruce A Stevens

First Edition

*The views expressed in this book are those of the author and do not necessarily
reflect those of The Salvation Army. All profits derived will be directed
towards supporting the international ministry of
The Salvation Army.*

Table of Contents:

Preface

FINDING HOW BEST TO SHARE my experience of corps officership with those closest to me is not an easy thing. When I have precious time with my two children, Kerry and Mitchell, I simply want to enjoy their company and 'do life' with them. At the same time, I want to do what I can as a father and Christian leader to help them as they engage in ministry.

Ministry in The Salvation Army is uniquely different from most other denominations of the Christian church. As a corps officer (pastor) you are appointed to a corps (church), yet that focus encompasses the whole community rather than merely those who are part of the local congregation. We are called to serve everyone without discrimination, which we do in partnership with highly engaged soldiers (activist members committed to our mission).

There are many new approaches to ministry taking place in these days, with officers and soldiers focused on making a transformational difference in their local community. These incarnational ministry methods are definitely having an impact for Jesus Christ and reflect the 'hands on' and 'can do' approach of the early Army. The Salvation Army's officers and soldiers historically were risk takers trying new ways to organically deliver the mission; the gospel demands we embrace this approach in every generation. Whilst ongoing innovation is essential, the heart of ministry will naturally always be about how we respond to and care for people.

The corps I served at had strong attractional frameworks to their ministry, providing a range of programmes and services for the broader community. Living out our mission and holistically sharing the gospel will always be our focus and to this day, many corps continue to effectively use attractional methods as well as organically reaching into the community. Irrespective of how we do ministry, basic principles of leading and caring for people apply in whatever context we may find ourselves serving.

In sharing my personal experiences of leading and caring for people, the majority of principles and practices are in reality common sense. I was certainly not the most contemporary and innovative leader of a Salvation Army Corps, yet God blessed the ministry in ways that exceeded my expectations and resulted in the lives of individuals being beautifully transformed.

Now that my precious 2 children are both in ministry at Salvation Army Corps, I have chosen to write about my leadership journey in the hope they will benefit from my experience. They find themselves in an ever changing world. I want them to think through how to minister in today's society in ways that will achieve transformational outcomes for the Kingdom of God. I want them to not stumble in areas where guidance can provide a clearer path. I want them to achieve every potential they have to be the very best disciples of Jesus Christ and effective leaders in The Salvation Army.

By sharing some of my own experiences including successes and failures, I am hopeful of stimulating their thinking. My prayer is they will discover for themselves how they can uniquely achieve their full potential in Christ.

My precious children, Kerry and Mitchell

I get to share my life with Debra, my best friend who understands me better than anyone else. She believes in me and when I am at my best, she is normally close by. I am grateful for the encouragement she gives me and the awesome wife, mother, grandmother and friend she consistently is.

'You are my servant';
I have chosen you and have not rejected you.
So do not fear, for I am with you;
do not be dismayed, for I am your God.
I will strengthen you and help you;
I will uphold you with my righteous right hand.
Isaiah 41:9-10 (NIV)

Foundations

TO BE CALLED BY GOD can be exciting and scary all at the same time. When you know officership is exactly what you must do in response to Christ's lordship of your life, it is a matter that demands our complete obedience. This is not a career choice, it's not about meeting the perceived expectations of others and it's certainly not about trying to fill a void in the absence of clarity about what really matters in life.

For me personally, a constant sense of calling has required my full obedience, including when things haven't been as I would like. I know others for whom there is no distinct calling from God, yet a compelling sense to offer themselves for full engagement in ministry as officers. There is an obvious difference here, yet I have seen officers come from both perspectives and serve with total dedication to the mission.

My own experience of calling was unforgettable and critical to me holding fast when logic suggested otherwise. To be blunt, why would anyone subject themselves to a lifestyle without control over their actual ministry engaged in, where they would live, who they would work with and a broad range of conditions you commit yourself to obediently follow? It seems illogical, yet that is exactly what so many Salvation Army officers have done over the years in response to the unmistakable call of God.

To be totally transparent, there have been brief moments when I considered what other options may be available to me outside of officership. Given my calling came in the form of such a memorable and unforgettable vision, these thoughts have quickly subsided in the context of my Officer's covenant.

In reality, my calling involved much more than just whether I would pursue officership in The Salvation Army. The thought of leaving my career that I had worked hard at was difficult to come to terms with; I didn't 'want' to be an officer for a range of reasons, yet there was no mistaking this was exactly what God required of me. It was this thought that became pivotal in my faith journey. If I was to seriously allow Jesus Christ to be Lord of my life – to have total control – then my faith demanded total obedience to whatever he asked of me.

It did take some time to finally surrender myself after trying to 'do some deals' with God, yet I eventually accepted I needed to obey. It was futile trying to organise God and deep down, I knew I felt compelled to do exactly as He had called me to do.

My experience has been those who have an unmistakable calling from God are far more likely to cope in those extremely difficult times. In the absence of a 'call', those who are particularly disciplined, focused and with a strong faith have the greatest likelihood of surviving the challenge that officership is. Life is often unpredictable and circumstances occur that can impact on people being able to continue serving as officers; I am very conscious my focus needs to be on my own officership and support others in whatever situation they may find themselves.

The actual process of training for service as officers is just that - a process to equip you with a foundation for ministry. The goal is not to attend the School for Officer Training, rather it is commissioned officership. The place of ongoing development in varied ways continues and our Army provides many great opportunities, yet I remind you of the importance of being self-led leaders. You need wisdom to discern what training will assist and when the best time is to pursue it, considering your appointment dynamics and family needs in the context of your overall situation. This will be a life time process of continual learning in response to the community needs of the day.

Never forget that which is distinctive about officers as compared to the many highly committed soldiers we serve with. The call of God is upon us all and we are all faced with the choice of how we will respond to that specific plan for our life. I think of Dr John Philpot who is a loyal committed soldier at Warrnambool Corps and served the community exceptionally well as a Medical Practitioner. His service was a blessing to so many and he showed Christ's love in a practical way that was indeed ministry. This was a God ordained pathway for him that he followed and he has certainly made an incredible difference over many years.

I recall several individuals who walked alongside me at Perth Fortress Corps. They were great soldiers for whom nothing was too much trouble; willing servants consistently living out their faith and using their gifts as part of the body of Christ. Why do I highlight this? We say we believe in the priesthood of all believers, yet seemingly differentiate too often between officers and soldiers, as well as between soldiers with differing God given gifts. At the moment our language, practices or behaviour doesn't uphold this foundational value of our Army, we need to refocus. When we truly come under the lordship of Christ, every individual is a force to be deployed for mission with enormous potential that is uniquely theirs to live out.

What differentiates officers from soldiers is not our commitment, competence or character. When soldiers are passionately and totally committed to the mission, they achieve incredible outcomes for the kingdom. The major difference between officers and soldiers is their availability to accept appointments wherever God's mission may require.

We are soldiers of our Army before we are officers – it is vital we never forget this foundational matter.

The two of us as newly commissioned officers pictured in Kaniva, our first appointment.

Early Lessons

I CAN'T PRETEND THE TRANSITION from my secular employment to officership was easy. The path to get there included 2 years at the School for Officer Training and I am reassured to know cadets are trained very differently now. I could share much about my experience, albeit that is history and it is more appropriate to simply affirm the approach embraced by the current Training Principal and his team.

After commissioning I found myself, with Debra, leading in the remote communities of Kaniva, Broughton, Bordertown, Nhill, Yanac plus a number of other communities at Red Shield Appeal time. The contrast from working in professional corporate offices in the Melbourne central business district to Kaniva was extreme. I was out of my comfort zone and found myself wondering what I had got myself into. I recall vividly preaching on my first Sunday at the 2.30pm meeting at the Yanac Outpost with a small group of faithful believers whilst the sweat dripped down my back on a 42 degree day with no air conditioning; what in the world was I doing I wondered to myself.

That evening we had our official installation at the Broughton outpost (as it was then) and this was an experience no one could prepare you for. The township of Broughton consisted of one intersection with The

Salvation Army hall, Uniting Church (now no longer there) and the Community Hall. There was one house next to the Community Hall and the Country Fire Station next to the Uniting Church. As the time for our welcome meeting came near, we watched with great interest as cars approached and by the time worship was underway there were more than 50 people present. The township may have been small, but the people were absolutely incredible with those living on farms forming a strong community.

It didn't take long to realise the people throughout this region were wonderful and I quickly grew to love them. I certainly wouldn't compare this appointment with overseas service, yet adopting a missionary approach was required. So much of normal life was foreign to me including how people shopped, spent their recreational time, spent their money and even how they observed the Sabbath. For example, I quickly learnt that most places I was billeted at on Sundays did not cook on Sundays and a cold salad would be the meal of the day. There would certainly be no television and on recollection, there were a number of families who didn't even own a television.

I was to learn a great deal from these people and on reflection, I realise how natural and instinctive pastoral ministry became for me during these years. Having appropriate programmes was certainly important and helpful for the worshipping community, yet my own ministry was surprisingly (to me at least) very effective when personally investing in people. I became quite confident at quickly getting to the point and talking about spiritual matters, sometimes whilst spending a day working alongside the men of the corps.

There are some very precious memories I have of trying to drench sheep, driving headers and especially opening and closing gates repetitively. I even remember a day in Trevor Smith's truck carting grain; what a man of faith he was who went to be with the Lord at such an early age. A not so pleasant memory was breaking several ribs (it made a great story at the time) when I got a touch too excited working with David Dickinson for a day, yet these were great times of learning and ministry. I could also tell stories about my tractor driving, which was a source of amusement for some of the farmers watching my not so straight lines behind me.

This setting demanded a very different approach to the stereotypical image I had of pastoral ministry. Not only did I learn a great deal in those 4 years and enjoy unique times on farms, my own faith was strengthened and I sensed it was also helpful for those I ministered to. If I had gone and imposed my predictable template of how a pastoral visit should occur, I seriously doubt the same outcomes would have eventuated. Indeed this was a unique situation that demanded a similarly unique response.

My cadet experience had actually dampened my confidence, likely more to do with me than solely about the training process. Whatever the reason, it took me several months to feel confident again to lead boldly, although I must admit I did make a fairly significant decision on my second day in the appointment. I recall the language I shared in my most positive approach effectively said, "This will never happen again - we will find a solution". Yes I know the mantra is you shouldn't make an important decision straight away, to which I would add the words "unless it would be foolish not to". I soon rediscovered my confidence and relished the opportunity to lead.

Although most people were quite relational and willingly served very faithfully, it became very evident they were certainly eager to be led. Over the years I have received much feedback about the way I engaged the Corps Council and Senior Pastoral Care Council (Senior Census Locals as it was in those days).

When we gathered the corps leaders together for those early meetings, it took some time for them to realise I really meant it when I said we needed to lead together as the spiritual leaders of the corps. We weren't unduly quick to make decisions, rather we built a mutual confidence and trust that saw them enthusiastically support a range of new initiatives I eventually presented. They were great days and great people to minister alongside!

I could share stories about both Warrnambool and Perth Fortress where I also served that have very different contexts, yet with very similar themes in how we pursued ministry - particularly pastoral ministry - in culturally appropriate ways. Our focus should never be fixed on a specific method, rather we must always determine our strategy based on the missional outcomes we want to be achieved.

There were many practical lessons learnt about preaching, property maintenance and the power of prayer at my first appointment. These held Debra and me in good stead for our subsequent ministry and we continued to build on those lessons. You don't forget when miracles happen as a result of prayer or when amazing cultural change takes place when people work together on shared goals and projects.

One formative experience for us was when we needed to go without our weekly allowance on several occasions. The corps had insufficient funds to pay all our accounts and I recall the concern of our Assistant Treasurer, Jim Pye, when he realised he wouldn't be writing a cheque for the officers. I am very pleased officers don't live with this pressure in Australia these days, yet there were ways in which this was character building for us. I would also add it was character building for the corps as well in taking financial responsibility.

Everyone worked hard to see the corps flourish and be financially independent with an occasional small grant from DHQ to assist our budget. We were very well provided for and God continued to supply our very needs, both personally and for the corps mission.

Interestingly, the corps appointment that most fully utilised my gifts and passion was Warrnambool. The dynamic of a growing healthy worshipping community and an extensive range of corps managed social programmes fitted me 'like a hand in a glove'. My leadership of teams was refined in this appointment and I was particularly empowered by one Divisional Commander who entrusted me with various responsibilities in the region. I am very much indebted to Lieut. Colonel Barbara Perry for the trust she showed in me during those exciting and rewarding years.

It is no surprise that I read more books during those years at Warrnambool than I ever had, plus I was a regular conference attender and listened to leadership 'cassettes' as they were in those days. That discipline also continued particularly during my time at Perth Fortress, as well as embracing several opportunities for advanced leadership training through the Willow Creek Association.

The Warrnambool corps was blessed by a number of passionate and competent local officers, some of whom continue to serve to this day. A great blessing was to have Doug Baudinette as our Corps Treasurer. Doug readily assumed the additional responsibility of oversighting the corps thrift shop and also played an important support role with our social ministries run from the corps administration centre. Here was a leader for whom nothing was too much trouble and he was a great supporter of Debra and me. Doug was in his last 60's when ministering alongside us and could easily have chosen to retire in a more complete sense. He saw the possibilities of what the local corps could do and be and I found him a tremendous practical support in managing a wide range of issues, especially with the corps thrift shop.

What was a new challenge at Warrnambool for me personally was the importance of balancing my focus between management and practical ministry. I know all too well that administrative leadership and management play an important part in our Army's ministry, whether that is as corps officers, social programme officers or chaplains. Yes that is important and legitimate ministry, yet as a corps officer I would remind myself this was merely about the framework that facilitated all our corps did to minister. For me, what worked was clarifying for myself and communicating to key leaders and staff what my strategy to manage was.

I spent two full days in the office each week when I did all administration, had weekly staff management meetings, met with staff for accountability purposes and general corps matters. I devoted a whole day each Wednesday at home to preparing for two meetings on Sunday and invested one day and various nights in pastoral ministry. That left a full day for those things that hadn't quite been finished during the week (Saturday) and obviously Sunday was a full day with two meetings plus prayer meeting and other programmes.

During these 4 years at Warrnambool, I developed a memorable framework to help hold myself accountable for how I proactively invested my time. This was the era of my 'P' days, which was a source of great amusement for some. Here is how it worked; Monday was my play day, Tuesday was a programme day, Wednesday was my preparation day, Thursday was a pastoral ministry day, Friday was another programme day, Saturday was procrastination day (for those things I hadn't quite got finished) and Sunday was my platform and preaching day. Whilst I didn't widely share this, I found it helpful in managing my diary and planning ahead.

Whilst many people say it is the worst day to have off, I loved to have Monday as my day off. That worked really well for Debra and me and I relished Sunday nights when there was a sense of completion after the week (I saw the week going from Monday to Sunday). There were occasions when we were unable to have our usual day off due to divisional events, funerals, etc., yet I saw this as being fair considering there were many Saturdays when I only needed to work half a day.

There were situations when I got things quite wrong in those early years, yet experience is often the most powerful teacher we can have. I am pleased we have embraced a more professional and safe approach to ministry in these days, albeit there are some situations you can never prepare for or anticipate. This is when you simply have to strive to be solutions focused and do the best you can; this is often the lot of an officer in an unpredictable world. I certainly learnt some helpful lessons in those early years, and often did so the hard way.

I remember responding to a call for help in Kaniva from a man who was distraught and potentially suicidal, asking me to go and spend time with him to talk. My response was instinctive and I soon arrived and was welcomed into the man's home, only to sit down in his lounge and have him sit opposite me and pick up a loaded shotgun from the ground. He held that shotgun throughout our discussion. I recall I didn't actually feel scared as such, but was naturally uneasy and very concerned for him.

Once I had left after quite some time and amazingly having opportunity to pray with him, I came to realise the serious nature of the situation and that I should have taken someone else with me. I also felt I could have done a far better job of asking more appropriate questions initially on the phone to get a more complete sense of the situation. Now that I look back all these years later, I certainly should have asked far better questions and if I had realised he had a gun, this would clearly have been a police matter.

Another unpleasant Kaniva experience was taking a parcel of food to a family on a farm, only to be literally attacked by a pack of dogs as I approached the house. I was bitten and it was extremely terrifying for me. When the lady I was going to see came outside to see what had happened, she didn't believe I had been bitten and told me to take my "#%?!" food parcel and go away. People found it hard to believe this really happened to me, but I can certainly remember the doctor insisting on a tetanus injection after seeing the bite marks. Maybe this helps explain why I don't like being near dogs these days!

For me, there were many lessons learnt from experience that have shaped how I then ministered. It obviously isn't pleasant when things don't go as you anticipate, yet there are never any guarantees of an easy journey in ministry. There will always be ongoing challenges and messy times, yet God has a way of continually presenting opportunities to share His love and grace to those He brings across our path. These can be times of great joy right through to the other extreme when people are struggling with incredible sadness and loss.

Given the death of someone is such a great time of need, I always responded positively when asked to conduct a funeral whenever I could accommodate it. Such ministry is fundamental to caring and having been appointed to the community - not solely the local corps - it was a priority to respond to need in 'my patch'. I can only recall a few times in all my officership when other commitments could not be rearranged to allow me to serve. Not surprisingly, there were many wonderful ministry opportunities that arose.

As I have reflected on my early years, it is interesting how many memories flood back of supporting families in times of loss. There were some tragic instances of unexpected death where it was an incredible privilege to minister to those grieving. I shared with families who found hope through their experience of God's plan for our salvation and sadly also in circumstances where people struggled with no understanding of real hope at all. I quickly learnt to always be ready for the unexpected in conducting funerals and you could say I have seen it all; how interesting that most officers have quite a range of stories they can tell about what has happened at funerals.

I am aware there are some officers who find funerals a challenge to conduct, whereas I saw them as a great mission opportunity. Yes, it can take great sensitivity and grace when there has been a tragic death from an accident or suicide, yet whatever the situation we are given the privilege of sharing Christ. In reality, I always preach the gospel in a way I sense will be appropriate for the occasion and have never felt any qualms about that. It could be easy to feel a need to adopt a 'fresh approach' in how you conduct a funeral, yet the gospel is the gospel. However you do it, simply focus on the people there and confidently preach Christ!

When thinking about those early years, it warrants mention that prior to officership it was not uncommon to leave home early in the morning and have little time in the evening before leaving for corps activities. On some days, I would need to go straight from the office to a rehearsal or meeting. These experiences proved significant and I never forgot about this when considering asking corps members to attend an evening meeting.

By contrast, corps officership provided us with incredible flexibility and I was able to share in special occasions with our children that would never have been possible as a corporate tax consultant. The hours are certainly long as an officer, yet there is enormous scope to manage your time that many people simply don't have in their daily occupation.

Those first two appointments – both 4 years – were tremendous times of blessing for me personally. There was so much to learn, but what an exciting time it was to be an officer entrusted to minister in local communities. I still remember those days with great affection, both in terms of the actual serving and particularly as I think of the individuals I was privileged to minister to.

Being a corps officer is certainly a great privilege and incredibly rewarding.

The family outside Broughton Hall, a place of great memories for us.

General Leadership

EVERY LEADERSHIP SCENARIO WILL PRESENT challenges that can seem overwhelming at the time, yet are really just another situation requiring problem solving at a different level. I found a combination of attending seminars, reading books and life experience all worked together to help mould my approach to leadership. Together with an evolving strength of character shaped by my faith journey, this all worked to develop greater resilience to manage when things became messy. Let there be no doubt, one of the certainties of being a corps officer is there are plenty of uncomfortable situations to deal with. They can't be avoided, they won't be enjoyable and learning to manage them in a leader like manner is imperative to be a successful Godly corps officer.

I often hear people talking about the seemingly low level of resilience amongst young leaders these days. What I also hear people saying is this is definitely not a unique Salvation Army issue, rather it is a generational challenge. Whilst this may be hard to hear, it is an issue that cannot be ignored. A colleague officer recently shared about talking with a senior officer of the Australian Defence Forces who stated this same problem exists for them. I also wonder whether the issue is not always merely about resilience when things are difficult, yet is sometimes about an individual's work ethic when there is much to be done with a resultant impact on lifestyle.

This latter issue of work ethic is something where I accept my own approach is sometimes unhealthy in terms of self-care. It occurs to me the level of engagement and hours worked that can be healthily sustained will naturally differ for people depending on a wide range of factors. Having said that, we can never forget that officership is about self-sacrifice. The covenantal relationship we enter into is not based on a normal employment contract with entitlements that are guaranteed.

Reflecting on how resilience is developed, I learnt many life lessons when I was younger which Debra and I strive to instil in those under our influence. Things like 'if you start something you need to see it through' and 'if something is worth doing it's worth doing well' may seem old fashioned adages, yet they articulate and help develop values and character. We certainly lived by these values in our childhood ourselves as modelled by our parents and constantly exposed our own children to these same values.

Might I suggest this theme even extends to the practice of basic manners; saying thank you, looking people in the eye when you speak to them, helping with tasks without needing to be asked and being an exceptional team player are not always the custom these days. These are basic life skills that are formed in our childhood as they are modelled, taught and caught in the home.

As an example, I find it disappointing the lack of practical care I have been shown on occasions when accepting an invitation to speak at a corps. In my time as a Divisional Secretary, I would sometimes not so subtly let corps officers know what arrangements would be appropriate to make in preparation for a visit from divisional or territorial guests. When you invite guests to minister at your corps, do all you can to anticipate their needs including greeting them on arrival, providing a safe place for any valuables they may have, ensuring water is available during the meeting and generally ensuring they feel like special guests.

How we can assist young leaders to grow resilience is a question we need to keep asking. I would like to think they would also be eager to pursue what this looks like and what has shaped those who demonstrate it. One book that was particularly helpful for me was 'Courageous Leadership' by Bill Hybels. Many of the concepts addressed in his book resonated loudly in my mind and were most helpful to help me persist and retain focus.

A great lesson I learnt from Bill Hybels was that in times of crisis, people will look to their leader who has enormous scope to influence the response and attitude of all. In the midst of challenge, a positive mission focused perspective can permeate those feeling downhearted and instil hope. It's a fact of life that people will often take their lead from the key leader. That means when a crisis is taking place, the role of the leader will be pivotal in shaping the mindset and resultant response of the corps.

My personal leadership journey has been interesting at times. Ministry as a corps officer was a great fit for me and I absolutely relished divisional leadership with Debra. These appointments gave me scope to truly lead within those spheres of influence and God's blessing shone through in many ways. We saw people come to faith, be discipled and step up to engage in leadership in a wide range of ways.

The value of local officership is something we both passionately believe in, reflective of our Army's emphasis on the priesthood of all believers as I mentioned earlier. We saw great outcomes from releasing and empowering local officers to lead in corps settings and they knew we would back them through thick and thin.

We had been well served by a hardworking Corps Sergeant Major at Perth Fortress Corps who stepped aside after he had served for a number of years. We initially struggled to identify who might be the best person for this key role, knowing how critical it was in our continuing mission strategy. After prayerfully reflecting and speaking with other corps leaders, we eventually sensed the direction we should be pursuing. What became evident was the best person for the job was someone we had assumed may not be interested in the role. We needed someone who had a strong relationship with Christ, was respected within the corps, understood how to lead and had the benefit of wisdom in decision making and communicating with people on challenging subjects.

There are two lessons to be learnt from this. Firstly, it is not wise to make assumptions about how people will respond to a request. We knew John Robinson was the right person for the job and it was appropriate we allowed him to decide if he was willing to take on the challenge. I can still vividly recall visiting him and his wife, Lenie, to put the challenge to them and sensing the Holy Spirit had been at work ahead of us.

Secondly, I realised first-hand the truth that high capacity people are more likely to accept a significant assignment with scope for major impact. John had proven over the years he was highly competent as a leader/manager and accepted the challenge to help our corps be the best we could be. We were to benefit greatly from his leadership in many ways, but never more than the way he would accept responsibility and manage matters of conflict that would otherwise have become our lot. The lesson learnt was high calibre people are worthy of high calibre requests.

My 8 years at Perth Fortress were a challenging and exciting time. There were many significant matters needing to be considered and decisions made, as well as more trivial things that weren't important to the mission but detracted from the main game. I can recall a number of such matters but shall resist sharing the details about those who got worked up about not much at all. John and several other key leaders would embrace the challenge and tackle issues head on, keeping us informed as needed.

One example I can share was when we started having young adults start coming to worship at Perth Fortress wearing baseball caps. When someone had a 'whinge' about the youth of the day, John would respond with vision soaked language reminding those complaining how wonderful it was to have them at worship - cap and all. John modelled how you could respond to most petty concerns using a version of your basic 'stump speech' with vision and mission at the heart of it.

Throughout my corps officership, I was led by 7 different Divisional Commanders over 16 years (3 in Western Victoria and 4 in Western Australia). There was not one who didn't support me in my leadership and I speculate the way I endeavoured to keep them informed about key matters helped develop trust. There were several occasions where we saw a particular issue very differently, yet rather than allow frustration to grow I would make an appointment to talk through the matter to ensure I had been heard and seek to resolve the tension as best as possible. The outcome wasn't always what I wanted and on occasions, I discovered there was a better way to view a matter I had thought I knew best about.

I actually recall contacting Divisional Headquarters when I was at Kaniva Corps and making an appointment to visit Ballarat that very day, involving a 3.5 hour drive each way. All these years later, it is interesting that I don't even recall the specific matter which I obviously thought was quite significant at the time.

Any Divisional Headquarters team naturally wants every corps to flourish and I also did all I could as a corps officer to be a great supporter of divisional events. That same logic resonated with me when I was a divisional officer and I made every effort to be a great soldier at my local corps (this has not been as easy as a Territorial Cabinet member travelling the territory).

We all know that grass roots ministry is the foundation of all we do. As a divisional officer, I believed my default position when considering new initiatives needed to be 'how can I help this happen'. That doesn't mean the answer was always yes – far from it – yet I would hope those I worked with would affirm my passion to be a creative facilitator of mission.

I have really enjoyed investing in other leaders over the years and relished working with cadets and candidates in corps settings. For me, it reflects that I am seemingly better as a consultant practitioner than a teacher in the true sense. Whilst they were with me, I treated them as colleagues in ministry including all the privileges and expectations I would have of a colleague officer. I unapologetically pushed them based on my assessment of their potential and saw some really exciting outcomes. At the time, some believed I pushed a touch hard yet in later years have thanked me and joked about some of the creative 'games' we would play to teach them lessons.

One of the areas I often received affirmation in was my willingness to have honest conversations with people and openly provide constructive feedback. This proved to be quite pivotal in my ministry at Warrnambool and Perth Fortress, where I was heavily reliant on paid and volunteer staff being at their very best. My subsequent ministry as a Divisional Commander also particularly demanded the use of these skills to help officers reach their full potential and support the overall mission objectives of the territory.

In those early years, there was a time when I was becoming increasingly frustrated when week after week an issue was not receiving attention by the staff team. I recall being confronted yet again with another week of inaction and found myself pausing momentarily in the staff meeting to consider why this was happening. In my time as Divisional Commander of the Western Victoria Division, I was reminded by one of those staff members what I did to resolve the situation and 'send a message' about my expectations.

I chose to instantaneously call the meeting to a halt and thus free up the next hour for the matter to be dealt with immediately. I then confirmed the availability of staff that afternoon for a further meeting where they would provide a report on the progress made. Apparently my language was gracious, yet very clearly conveyed my expectation that matters be actioned in a timely way.

As I reflect on how I engage with people, I am aware some people can actually find me somewhat threatening at times. One leader I have invested in over many years would joke about dealing with me and was heard to say "Be afraid … be very afraid" when talking about meeting with me. Whilst she shared this in a spirit of respect and joked about me being 'scary', there was nonetheless a kernel of truth I couldn't ignore. Finding the balance between challenging people to be their best requires an assessment of their competence, balanced by their emotional capacity to hear the truth at that specific time.

Like many life disciplines, discerning how transparent to be with staff is therefore a never ending balancing act. My experience is you need to be constantly evaluating how best to speak into people's lives and accept you won't always strike the perfect balance. Personally, I would prefer to err on the side of being transparent and sharing what I see in others rather than take a conservative approach and ignore the obvious. Too often, I sense leaders abdicate responsibility to speak words of truth in preference to trying to be 'friends' with those under their influence.

Even when feedback is graciously shared in a spirit of love, it naturally remains difficult to hear and I am no different to anyone else. Having said that, I would prefer to be engaged in a discussion about my ministry performance than have it ignored should I be failing in an area.

People make their own choices about how they respond to feedback and whilst they may initially find it quite confronting, I have on numerous occasions eventually been thanked for sharing my observations. Self led leaders are eager to receive feedback and be held accountable for their ministry effectiveness. Interestingly, I recall a senior leader sharing with me his observation that some officers say they wish to be held accountable … until they actually are. To be the best officers and soldiers we can be requires us to readily embrace constructive feedback, especially when it comes from respected colleagues.

There were times when I found myself making assumptions about people who found themselves in roles they were not gifted or effective in, merely because they agreed to serve to fill a ministry void. I recall challenging underperforming local officers based on my assessment of how God had gifted them to serve, only to discover they would happily step aside if there were other options more suited to their spiritual gifts and talents. This requires much diplomacy and vision based messaging to ensure people realise you truly value them and want to see them succeeding in what they do, in addition to the obvious missional outcomes required for your corps to be effective.

I do need to stress there are some occasions where leadership requires decisive action and messaging. There have been times when I have needed to terminate the ministry of people as a result of their failure to adhere to The Salvation Army's values or consistent failure to meet agreed performance standards. In the case of paid staff, I have always appreciated the wisdom and support of divisional leadership and in particular, Human Resources practitioners who have coached me. Where a culture exists of regular engagement that openly shares feedback, a difficult performance based discussion becomes much easier to manage in the context of an established paradigm of honesty.

On reflection, there have been times when I have needed to heed the warning that I can come across as 'scary'. That means working hard at listening well, checking that my body language is relaxed, asking appropriate questions so I can better understand people's feelings and carefully deciding if the time is right for that 'one key question' or if it needs to wait for another day.

I would also add there are times in leadership when it serves me well to be 'just a little bit scary' when a key message is not being heard or someone is not accepting responsibility in their leadership. As I write, I can hear my dear friend saying "Be afraid … be very afraid" and to be honest, I remind myself my greater objective is to be the best leader I can be rather than the best friend I can be.

There is no mistaking the fact that to be a relevant competent leader, you need to be continually reinventing yourself to some degree. A significant investment is made by The Salvation Army in facilitating ongoing training for officers and soldiers through the Catherine Booth College. Whilst I have not undertaken any formal study in recent years, I certainly worked very hard to develop myself throughout my years as a corps officer.

One of the reasons I feel equipped to write about my experiences is the knowledge the essential framework of Christian ministry never changes, only the methods of the day change. We will always need to be ensuring our personal relationship with Christ is current and vibrant, be reliant on the power available in prayer and continually be responding to people's holistic needs. These foundational matters don't change, yet there will regularly be new challenges requiring new skills.

We arranged for family photos to be taken at a 'Family Festival Weekend' at Broughton. Those photos have continued to surface in many and varied ways ever since.

Being a Good Follower

MANY GREAT LEADERS HAVE SHARED about the importance of being a great follower if you ever hope to be an effective leader. Like many officers I knew this in my heart, but it is only in practice that it becomes reality. I have had experiences where I have struggled to be at my best with some leaders, yet I have certainly excelled under the influence of highly effective leaders.

Jesus is our model and he willingly submitted himself by allowing John the Baptist to baptise him. There is sometimes a real tension to lead boldly whilst humbly allowing yourself to be led, this being a classic challenge for 'second chair' leaders.

When everyone is working to the same goal and people's gifts are used to maximum effect, the issue of leading and following can fade into obscurity. I love Commissioner Floyd Tidd's language when he says we should be pursuing the 'best fit for mission' for everyone. Imagine what it would be like if every officer and soldier was truly using their God given gifts; imagine the exponential ministry outcomes that could be achieved for the kingdom.

During my time as the divisional secretary in Western Australia, I found myself under the leadership of Commissioner Todd Bassett for several months. Here was a leader who arrived and together with his wife,

Commissioner Carol Bassett, immediately demonstrated trust in Debra and me, treating us as colleague leaders. They are incredibly experienced officers and Todd had been the National Commander of The Salvation Army in the USA prior to retirement.

Whilst it was obvious they would be very reliant on us, it quickly became evident it was in their nature to work very collaboratively. We were consulted, listened to, involved in key meetings and included in the actual process of decision-making. Personally, I found this both empowering and engaging and he certainly was able to get the best out of me as he led the division.

By contrast, it can be disempowering when consultative decision-making is in reality a process of information sharing. Leaders certainly need to be willing to make hard decisions and it is appropriate to simply share the background and context, rather than seemingly consult in the knowledge a decision has already been reached. The lesson for me is to openly declare decisions made where circumstances have required determinative action to be taken.

Working with Todd and Carol was a great example of how commitment to a shared vision with the best use of people can be incredibly energising and productive. How blessed we are to have opportunities to do this on a daily basis wherever we are. As a corps officer, you have the privilege and responsibility to get the best out of your local leaders for the sake of the mission.

Being a good follower means you need to give your best on a consistent basis. There is no place for half-hearted efforts or sulking because you don't get your own way. There have been times when I have got this wrong and I vividly recall an incident at Perth Fortress where I was guilty as charged.

In my early months at the corps, I found myself playing in the brass band and receiving some critical comments at a rehearsal I believed were unfair and delivered harshly (not from the bandmaster I should add). I am not the worst player in Salvation Army bands and found myself very annoyed at what had happened. My response was akin to sulking by putting in minimal effort for the rest of the rehearsal. That night I arrived home angry knowing what I was capable of and feeling I had been treated unjustly.

The next day I realised that irrespective of how I had been treated, I had let myself and my leader down. It was a rather humbling thing to do, yet I knew I needed to meet with the leader to apologise and commit to give my best. The way I had responded was simply unacceptable and had someone responded to my leadership in this way, I likely would have wanted to gently challenge them. My recollection is that leader was quite stunned with my admission and it likely helped advance the relationship we were to develop over those years and which has continued to this day.

Be assured, I don't always get it right and I know deep within when I am not giving my best. In those times, I remind myself of the biblical mandate to do everything as for the Lord and rise above whatever feelings I may have. It is in such leadership situations when resilience and emotional intelligence become incredibly important.

As leaders, we need to set the culture of how to be a good follower to those within our sphere of influence and relying on our leadership.

Pictured in the 'board room' at Warrnambool Corps,
which also doubled as Debra's office.

Leading as a Couple

AT THE RISK OF GENERALISING, it is so often the case that God puts together people with complementary personalities and skill-sets. My own case is one where Debra complements my weaker areas and I complement hers. There are some crossovers where we may occasionally be butting heads and thankfully we have always seemed to find a way to navigate these.

Critical to working well is releasing each other to work within strengths, albeit you can't afford to totally ignore all work areas. A good example is the need to develop a basic level of administrative acumen and skills to manage in officership. This has never been a strong point for Debra, yet in recent years she has progressively grasped concepts and basic skills to function reasonably well.

Whilst in an appointment together such as corps officership, it is far easier to release each other in those areas of strength. Debra is currently in a predominantly administrative leadership appointment, requiring more developed skills in that area. The good news is she has progressively grown in this area, yet it would be foolish to think it comes easy to her now.

When any of us tackle tasks in areas we are not naturally gifted in, it will take significant emotional energy and you need to acknowledge and allow for that. Salvation Army

Officership is not about picking and choosing what we would like to do; tasks are required to be fulfilled and we need to find solutions to ensure required outcomes are achieved (which often involves utilising others gifted in those areas).

Most of us like to have clarity about what we are responsible for and that has certainly been the case for Debra and me. What worked for us was coming to agreement about what we would focus on and then empowering each other to assume responsibility.

I recall a time at Perth Fortress when we sensed God's leading to place particular investment in our children's ministries. I was carrying a significant load and we agreed Debra would take on this role in an all-encompassing way. For this to work, I needed to constantly remind myself to get out of the way and let her lead, which meant needing to regularly remind people who the key person was. The outcomes were tremendous both in terms of ministry and helping Debra and I invest our times effectively. Added to this, there was the joy it brought Debra to be leading in an area where she had real passion and involved focused engagement with a range of leaders and stakeholders.

There are some things that don't get talked about but should, so let me outline a few obvious ones. When we lead worship together, we commit to each other to be attentive to the extreme. There are no wandering eyes, yawning, fidgeting, etc. We keep eye contact and focus on whichever one of us is upfront.

We never 'talked shop' in front of our children. Let me say that again, we **never** 'talked shop' in front of our children. I trust you get the message.

Following Sunday meetings, we would do our utmost to be at the door or at morning tea and shake every hand. We wanted to connect with everyone and not be seen talking with a small group of people off to the corner; if that ever happened it was when most people had gone home. There were times when we literally ran down the road at Perth Fortress to connect with someone who had slipped by, such was our determination to link with people.

When it came to strategic meetings such as Corps Council and other special purpose meetings, we would normally have 'the meeting before the meeting'. The purpose certainly wasn't to predetermine the outcome; rather it was to ensure we knew where each other stood on matters so we wouldn't be surprised. In those discussions, Debra would suggest that occasionally some of her greatest ideas would have become mine by the time our meeting took place. Whether it was inspired leadership by her or me merely allowing her to express what I knew she would eventually get to understand is a matter still unresolved to this day.

We would also discuss practical details of how we would structure our meetings, even including where each of us would sit. This was important especially in our Corps Council meetings. The normal practice was to preferably sit in a circle – not at a table - and not be together or opposite each other. For example, if there were 9 seats in a circle one of us would sit in position 1 and the other in either position 4 or 6; call us pedantic if you wish, but our experience was small things like this made a difference to our leadership and helping everyone feel equally valued in the team.

Debra and I agreed that from a leadership perspective, we needed to have one key identifiable leader. Given our respective giftedness, it ended up that I played that role and Debra would willingly allow me to lead when we needed to make a decision on a matter. She would certainly express her view in that process quite strongly, yet it would be too problematic to try and provide ultimate leadership as a couple.

From my perspective, I was shown great trust and respect by Debra and I needed to do everything I could to demonstrate mutual trust and respect. Recognising the urgency of the gospel, the leadership mantle always sits quite heavily on your shoulder.

What also needs to be said is that as the key leader, I would meet regularly with staff and corps leaders. Not surprisingly, the day came when Debra declared "I want a meeting too" and for the remainder of our corps officership, an entry would regularly appear in the diary called 'Executive Meeting'. That sounds very impressive, doesn't it!

How we managed at home is a matter that warrants mention, being an area any couple need to master to be at their best. We could only survive personally and as a family if we both shared the various responsibilities in managing our home life.

From our first year at Kaniva, we agreed there would be days when I would be the one caring for the children and responsible for cooking our evening meal, amongst other routine essential chores around the house. All these years later, I now find myself regularly being the one who routinely does our grocery shopping.

Over the years, I have also done my share of housework fairly regularly and have always been the one responsible for family finances (surprise, surprise) and other things like the car and garden. Even now, I often cook and as I am writing recall that only last night I went home to prepare our meal, plus several other chores before Debra got home much later in the evening. It is important to understand these are **our joint responsibilities** and who undertakes them depends on the bigger picture of our respective workloads at the time.

The only way a couple can give their best is when there is mutual agreement not just about ministry responsibilities, but domestic responsibilities as well.

The key message about leading as a couple is I am a better leader because I get to 'do life' and ministry with Debra. That works well because we mutually accept responsibility and support each other.

This is one of my favourite pictures taken at Perth Fortress after a wedding I officiated at. Perth Fortress Corps was a place we came to love dearly and it was an incredible privilege to share in so many special moments with people. We saw lives changed!

Self Leadership

THERE IS MUCH THAT CAN be said about the importance of self leadership, yet for me the most critical factor over the years has been managing my holistic health. What is quite interesting is that in different seasons of my life, what I have needed has changed.

In my early ministry years the priority was on my spiritual development and developing the basic skills required to fulfil my role as an officer. As the years progressed, I found myself needing to quite aggressively enhance my leadership capacity and practice. It was in these years that I was very active in attending seminars, reading books and listening to teaching material. Maybe it is the way that I am naturally wired, yet it was quite affirming to discover much of what I learnt confirmed my common sense instincts of how to lead. By contrast, there were other areas where the learning curve was rather steep, particularly in the area of theology.

I found my needs changed quite dramatically when I moved from corps leadership to administrative leadership at divisional headquarters in Western Australia. It was a totally new experience to be a second chair leader and it took time to come to understand the dynamics of this role. The scope of the role was very broad and I actually found myself in tears one day sharing with the Divisional Commander of the day, Major Iain Trainor, about my inability to manage. On reflection, my expectations of myself were unrealistic and it is no surprise Iain affirmed and encouraged me.

I found the book 'Leading from the Second Chair' by Mike Bonem and Roger Patterson very helpful, as well as an interview recorded between Bill Hybels and Mike Bonem on the subject. There is a real art to being successful as a 'second chair' leader and it is far from straight forward. An officer leader who assisted me in exploring how to manage this tension was Commissioner Raymond Finger, who I learned from as I observed his approach to leadership.

My current appointment as Secretary for Business Administration sees me as a second chair leader (third chair in actual fact). My experience is you need to lead as if you have full authority, whilst exercising wisdom about those matters that the key leader will want to direct.

I have served as a second chair leader under 5 different leaders and whilst there are similarities between some of them, the bottom line is you need to accept it is impossible to always anticipate how they will wish an issue to be managed. Officers can find themselves appointed in assistant or associate roles as corps officers, hence this is not an issue solely for administrative leaders. Such situations highlight the importance of being a great follower, as referenced previously in chapter 5.

Most times I believe I get it right as a 'second chair' leader, yet occasionally I find myself surprised and you need to simply accept the decision and move on. Having said that, I can't pretend it's easy to do that if you sense the best decision is not being made. In such times, I remind myself that none of us can arrive at the best possible decision all the time and often there are major facts not openly shared for valid reasons. This latter point is particularly significant given there can be circumstances preventing all information from being openly shared; when this is the case you need to trust the judgement of your leader.

A recurring theme is the importance of resilience; experience has been my best teacher here, including watching other leaders manage in times of challenge. When leaders are under pressure, you get a free lesson in how they manage their emotions, their body language and how they express themselves. I have learnt to manage reasonably well, yet there are some 'hot buttons' I have that can evoke a response out of character for me if pushed hard enough. As you get older, you become more self-aware and more able to manage those buttons getting pushed.

Without a doubt, I need to set the bar higher in my tolerance level especially when I'm feeling emotionally drained. When I'm on top of things I tend to manage most situations reasonably well, yet if I happen to be feeling emotionally drained and physically tired I need to be extra cautious. Developing good self-awareness has been important for me and I am helped by Debra in this area.

Learning how best to lead and come to grips with my own idiosyncrasies has been quite a journey. According to the Myers Briggs personality test - which I have taken on a number of occasions - I find myself amongst only 1% to 2% of the population as an 'INTJ'. If you have interest in what that means for a leader managing as a second chair leader, the web contains a plethora of information on this. Given the challenge this has presented, I have gone to see a counsellor for several months on two occasions. This has helped to some degree, yet in reality only insofar as it relates to understanding how I operate and are perceived by others. It seems I am indeed a rather unique character!

I recall Debra and I attending a conference in our early years of ministry. It was run by Arch Hart and focused on managing stress in ministry. This was one of the best conferences we ever attended and we left having learnt two key lessons.

Firstly, we were encouraged to be multifaceted and develop interests outside of ministry to keep us balanced in the midst of stress. Secondly, we heard practical lessons about how to protect our marriage that we adopted for ourselves.

We set rules for ourselves about how we would deal with the opposite sex and honestly share with each other in those times we may feel awkward. As Arch Hart described it, it's not wise to figuratively walk along a cliff face saying "I'll never fall off the edge" and tempt fate. When dealing with the opposite sex, you need to have the fence set back with a suitable margin from the cliff for safety with the rule being you don't go over the fence. That way, there is at least some margin for error if an awkward situation arises and you find yourself unknowingly straddling the edge of the fence.

In practical terms, this has meant times when people have not been happy with how I have responded to them. There have been occasions when needy women have wanted to hug me; I have been particularly careful depending on the situation and environment and actually simply refused on occasions. When I have done this, I have done my best to explain why and that it would be a different situation if Debra was with me. Some people find this to be overly cautious, yet I stress this is only when I am dealing with needy women who are looking for acceptance beyond what is healthy. There have been occasions when women have not understood and thought I was uncaring and I have needed to accept that.

Another awkward situation is when women flirt inappropriately; that's when I tell Debra bluntly and she will stand by my side and make it very clear for all to see that she's my girl and I'm her man.

When it comes to overall self-care, I'm reminded that the week prior to the Arch Hart conference, I attended a Rick Warren conference on 'The Purpose Driven Church' attended by 700 Christian leaders. The next week we attended the Arch Hart conference at the same location and there were less than 30 in attendance. We found this quite telling about the value placed on self leadership and caring for yourself. By the way, a couple from our first appointment saw the conference advertised and decided to pay for us to attend. This was a tremendous blessing that has continued to have ongoing benefit for our ministry and marriage.

Managing my time is something I have done quite well I believe, although I am sure I would be found guilty of often working too many hours. What we did well during our corps officership and to a lesser extent in divisional appointments was regularly have a day off. Added to that is the discipline we have practiced all our married life of always going away for holidays. We have been blessed financially to be able to do that, having always managed our personal finances effectively.

In our early years of marriage and then throughout officership whilst our children were at home, we always had a budget that started with our tithe and provided for annual offerings as well. I can't speak highly enough of the value we receive from having good holidays away from our normal setting; it simply wouldn't work for us having holidays in the quarters as corps officers. It was for this reason we were disciplined in making an allocation in our budget for this purpose. The other aspect of planning for holidays is ensuring you identify suitable dates and incorporate them in your overall forward planning for the year.

The journey I have had to manage healthy wellbeing over the years has been quite up and down at times. Once I was in my late 40's and early 50's, I seemed to have finally come to grips with how best to manage this. Now at age 57, I would love to say I have it mastered yet there are always interesting surprises that come along. The keys for me require I embrace a holistic view of my wellbeing and consider my spiritual life, social life, emotional wellbeing and physical wellbeing.

Those who know me well will be aware I was first confronted with depression in my mid 20's. In those days and in the professional circles I found myself, it was trendier to talk about having 'burn out'. On reflection, the help I received was not what I needed and I was fortunately blessed with a wife who stuck by me and cared for me really well. I would get myself so worked up on occasions and stressed I would end up with extreme anxiety and chest pains, only to discover everything was fine and I was hyper-ventilating. To be fair, I was quite protective and didn't talk openly about what I was experiencing, so it wasn't easy for people to help me. They were different times and it seemed to be far easier to pretend all was well.

What I was to learn was that managing my emotional health was pivotal to my overall wellbeing. Nothing would see me lose perspective and lead poorly more than when I became depressed. My spiritual life has always tended to be quite stable and there have not been any times of crisis in my faith other than when I was first called; I love the Lord and enjoy a rich and growing relationship with Him.

As I think back to my earlier years managing depression, I had such strong life commands that I 'soldiered on' and covered it up for many years. Obviously, that is not a good thing. There were times when I felt at my lowest, yet God was still able to do the most amazing things as he worked through me. Predictably, I would often crash afterwards and need ample space to recover ready for what was next. Whilst all this was happening, there was never a time when I didn't fulfil the roles that were expected of me; maybe this gives a glimpse into my makeup and determination to see things through I start.

Things changed for the better when I met Dr Lachlan Dunjey. He is a general practitioner in Perth who had a particular interest in caring for those in ministry. He was an excellent Christian GP and was just what I needed to progressively care for myself better over those 11 years I lived in Perth. If I fast forward through the years that followed, there were two key things that now see me very consistently maintaining good emotional health.

Firstly, I started exercising. In Perth I joined a gym and also recommenced playing cricket. The cricket was initially more about having fun and hopefully being able to play for several seasons with my son, Mitchell. What I was to experience were amazing benefits such that I realised I was a better leader in cricket season than in football season. These days, I walk regularly and use an 'app' to hold me accountable for my own good; I tend to be somewhat competitive and have met my goal in each of the years I have used the 'app'.

Secondly, Lachlan helped me come to realise I was often quite hard on myself. There were times when the demands I faced whilst at Perth Fortress were overwhelming, especially when ministry challenges, family challenges and several personal physical health issues collided all at the same time. Progressively becoming far more self-aware about my emotional health and the triggers that set me back was incredibly helpful. Some of this was as basic as acknowledging to myself how I felt each day and what I needed to do if things weren't as they should be. In this time, I also came to embrace the philosophy that it is ok to feel overwhelmed when things actually are overwhelming. I owe a great deal to Lachlan who was a messenger from God for me.

Nurturing my relationship with Christ is something I tend to be consistently inconsistent at. There will be times when I read scripture very regularly and other times when I might only read once every few days, with a key theme then circling in my thoughts over coming days. Like many officers, I found preparing for preaching enhanced my spiritual life and I have needed to find ways to replicate that.

Given I love music and walk so often, I regularly listen to music and find this a great way to stimulate my prayer life and generate space for God to speak to me. I also find God surprises me with the places he gives me inspiration and that recently happened during a meeting in the THQ Boardroom. You just never know when God will grab your attention and compel you to meditate on a particular theme.

My additional ministry responsibilities as Executive Officer of the Melbourne Staff Band *(see the picture at the end of this chapter)* have also been a real blessing for me that I am thankful for. This has provided amazing ministry opportunities where God's anointing has been palpable, as well as providing a community of believers for me to share life with. As much as the major concerts and international touring stands out as memorable, it is actually the regular ministry at local corps that I cherish the most. Overall the combination of ministry opportunities, sharing life with a community of believers and being part of a great brass band has brought much joy to me.

When it comes to healthy self leadership, no one can do this for you. I am saddened to observe some colleagues struggling with basic issues of life and leadership and wonder how we can help them grasp essential principles and practices. I have been bold enough to share my concern with officers about their physical wellbeing, especially if it is impacting on their capacity to achieve their full potential.

At the heart of being our best is the responsibility all officers have to live a life of discipline and sacrifice, giving us a strong foundation to make soul winning the primary purpose of our lives. In the knowledge God promises He is always with us and will equip us for every task, I believe we are obligated to cooperate with Him to be our very best.

I am reminded of a prayer chorus that is so easily sung, but a great challenge to live out. We are called to daily make a concerted effort to ensure every 'thought' and every 'deed' reflects Jesus Christ and our life achieves every potential He has for us. I grew up singing this chorus and recently came to a fresh appreciation of the depth of its message whilst attending the International College for Officers:

> *To be like Jesus, this hope possesses me.*
> *In every thought and deed, this is my aim my creed.*
> *To be like Jesus, this hope possesses me.*
> *His Spirit helping me, like Him I'll be.*
>
> *(Gowans & Larsson)*

God helps us in this journey towards wholeness and holiness, yet we cannot escape the foundational requirement that we commit ourselves to this pursuit.

Ministry with the Melbourne Staff Band has not only provided tremendous ministry opportunities, but is also incredibly rewarding for me at a personal level. This picture was taken during one of the sessions of 'Boundless' when The Salvation Army celebrated 150 years of mission.

Prayer Foundation

THINGS HAVE CHANGED DRAMATICALLY SINCE I commenced as a corps officer in 1992 at Kaniva/Broughton. Those were the days before email was in vogue and the availability of social media was just a dream. That meant we used old fashioned methods to share prayer needs with our congregation. This was the era of telephone prayer chains, not only at the corps but across the division. How things have changed now we have a world of instant status updates, tweets, emails and SMS.

Some things never change and the power of people gathering for prayer has always been a key weapon for the Christian church. I was confronted by a situation in our early years of ministry and felt compelled to use prayer like a ballistic missile to tackle an issue of spiritual bondage I believed needed to be dealt with. God actually gave me a vision that was quite astounding and attention grabbing to the extreme. I knew we needed to gather together and pray for victory in the spiritual realms over this particular matter.

What took place shouldn't have surprised me, but it did. Christians from several local congregations joined together on a regular basis to pray for our community and against those things that may be hampering the work of God. Not only did we see some miraculous outcomes, the shared commitment to pray together was good for the unity amongst believers. This was incredible evidence of the power of prayer when God's people gather together.

That same situation had another surprising element. I was astounded to discover one of the traditional denominations spoke against me and actually encouraged people not to engage with me. There was one member of that congregation who struggled with this, knowing what The Salvation Army believed and chose to regularly attend the prayer meetings. I eventually had opportunity to speak with the minister and his wife and help them understand our theology and it was significant to have him attend our public farewell from the community.

Memories flood back of other wonderful answers to prayer, which were so practical in nature. One such occasion involved Debra praying for a way to replace the worn out seating in our lounge room at the quarters. We had received confirmation we would serve a further term at Kaniva/Broughton and I expressed some frustration about not having a comfortable seat to relax in. Debra heard my frustration and prayed a solution would be found.

The very next day – I stress the very next day - a brand new lounge suite was delivered to us by the Horsham officers, who unbeknown to us had partnered with the Warrnambool Corps to provide what they already sensed we needed. How amazing the timing was and how encouraged we were that others were interested in such a practical matter. That story could be repeated many times over in our appointment at Kaniva/Broughton, where a lack of ready resources saw us praying that God would provide.

Fast forward to our years at Perth Fortress and people would subscribe to email communiques I used to keep people up to date on events and prayer needs. This was the era when 24/7 prayer gained momentum and there was a renewed commitment to prayer at the corps. In those years, special weeks of prayer and 24 hour prayer gatherings were significant in the life of the corps and we celebrated answers to prayer.

One of the real blessings of the 24/7 movement was it introduced people to new ways of praying and connecting with God. Creativity came to the fore in these days at Perth Fortress with immersive experiences providing opportunity to come into the presence of God in a wide variety of ways. Because people naturally connect with God depending on their unique personality, the team worked hard to ensure many different options existed. One of my highlights was the year we had a tent erected in the main hall, where there were powerful encounters with God and each other in this sacred space.

Let there be no mistake; God answers prayers and miraculous life transformations take place! I recall the amazing way a lady called Hazel came to experience Jesus Christ in our time at Kaniva. Here was a lady who cried out to God when in the depths of despair and He met her need through the love and fellowship of the corps. What a powerful testimony of the Lord's work she had.

However you do it, there always needs to be a solid foundation of prayer at the corps. As was often quoted to me in my early ministry, prayer is not preparation for the battle – prayer is the battle!

Debra shares with Hazel on the day she was accepted as a soldier of The Salvation Army. Her story is a reminder of the miracles God is still doing.

Articulating Mission Focus

I FOUND ONE OF THE greatest leadership challenges at two of the corps I served at was having clarity about our mission. This is seemingly ridiculous to think any part of The Salvation Army would have such a struggle, yet it became important to ensure we were making good decisions about how we invested resources and time into opportunities.

I have never been a great fan of mission statements unless they actually impact on actual strategy and values, hence catchphrases that adorn walls and printed materials that mean nothing just plain annoy me. In one of those corps, it literally took years to sense God's specific leading and for the broader team, and ultimately the congregation, to arrive at the point where our mission could confidently be articulated. Once this framework was clear, our language encapsulated this thinking and was given sharp focus in our various communications.

What I find quite hilarious about vision and mission in our Army is there is absolutely nothing new; we are, after all, The **Salvation** Army. Surely we know the basic mission God has given us to pursue … or at least we should. I am reassured in these days to hear this logic being regularly expressed, yet as I mention above declaring a specific focus can help shape strategy and how resources are invested for the best outcomes.

Different people will be motivated in different ways and for me, what works best is articulating the mission outcomes being strived for. The Australian Southern Territory's four mission objectives resonate with me far better than painting a picture of the vision you want to see achieved (transforming lives, caring for people, making disciples and reforming society).

Whilst describing a vision of what we strive for can be powerful, I identify best with goals that help establish a cultural framework with a solid foundation from which mission will happen naturally. It may be I am splitting hairs and I accept people view these concepts in many and varied ways.

I mentioned about the corps where we clarified issues of language and this definitely helped me in my leadership. So often there would be situations arising where relying on what we had declared our mission objectives were provided context for decision making.

It also led to a range of 'mission phrases' developing I would find myself regularly using in dialogue with people. This was really helpful in challenging discussions where negative comments, actions or innuendo could be responded to with positive missional language. Those moments occasionally became enjoyable, responding to situations in this style and changing the whole focus and communication style by the language being used. I am not convinced everyone can grasp this easily, yet many leaders intuitively do this with great effect.

The responsibility and privilege of casting inspiring vision is something demanding our best efforts and commitment to. People need to be continually reminded about the urgency of the gospel and our potential to make a profound difference in our world as we share Christ. To do that effectively, we need to be personally experiencing the fullness of Christ and others need to sense our genuine passion and dedication to seeing the mission achieved.

Those we serve with will innately sense how God is working in our own lives and this will flow through in our leadership, not to mention the obvious issues of spiritual authority that cannot be ignored. This is not just about growing The Salvation Army but seeing the Kingdom of God flourishing in a world that craves for hope. I often remind myself that as much as I love The Salvation Army and know God has called me to ministry through it, the Kingdom of God is far more important.

To be able to clearly articulate and cast vision can make an enormous impact in leading your corps. As the key leader, this is your personal responsibility to help keep everyone focused – and when you think you've just done it, you need to accept it will very soon be time to do it again.

The work of vision casting will never be complete.

I recall this occasion speaking at a special celebration at Perth Fortress Corps. I would often set myself the challenge of speaking without notes, especially when people would be attending who don't normally come to worship. My efforts to 'stand and deliver' became a catchphrase I am still reminded of by family and friends.

Having been bored by many a preacher on too many occasions, I want to 'connect' with people and give them something to think about they will hopefully remember.

Pastoral Ministry

I WASN'T OVERLY POPULAR WHEN as a young Corps Sergeant Major at my home corps, I indicated I would not be able to take on a group of people as part of the new pastoral care system. It was an admirable objective to neatly categorise everyone and create a structure to make sure everyone had a carer. The problem from my perspective was there was only so much I could do, so if I was to do that, then what wasn't I going to do? To be totally honest, I was sceptical the real objective was to simply create a nice flow chart so we felt better about what was already being done and maybe there would be marginally more that resulted.

Caring for people is a vital ministry in any Christian community and my experience is it can't easily be 'staffed' out organisationally to tick the boxes. There are many ways to care and different people respond to varying methods of care.

Over the years I have dealt with people at one extreme who 'needed' the male officer to personally visit and pray with them for it to qualify as a legitimate pastoral visit right through to the most incredible mutual care spending time with fellow Christians sharing about our faith journey. When you sit with someone and share in their story, there's something very real that goes deep. Naturally there are those times requiring an urgent response in times of crisis, yet one shouldn't presume a formula based approach will always be best.

I have been amazed by some incredible missional outcomes achieved when God has used me in the context of ceremonies. What a privilege it is to sit with a couple preparing for marriage or about to dedicate their child. These are precious opportunities and I made no apologies for asking good questions to quickly get to what it is that really matters in life. In the case of dedications, this objective would particularly influence how I approached visits including what would be the best time and place where we could have a meaningful discussion.

Most times this always became a sacred encounter, yet I also had my share of situations where the formalities of the actual public ceremony became the focus when portraying the right image and impressing others seemed to be the dominant concern. You do what you can do and I always prepared myself to speak into the lives of couples on key life and faith issues.

In times of loss, people have welcomed me into their lives as we have shared grief with lifelong connections being made. Whilst there are times when pastoral ministry can be scheduled and appointments made, the death of a loved one demands an urgent response. Who the best person is to respond needs to be determined, yet there also needs to be accountability to ensure the right care is provided.

I am blessed with a wife who absolutely oozes her love of God and love for people. She is at her best when caring for and discipling others and God has powerfully worked through her over the years. As corps officers we accepted full responsibility for caring for the people within our sphere of influence at the corps and I learnt a great deal from her.

What we have surprisingly observed over the years is pastoral ministry appears to be receiving less personal priority amongst colleague officers. It is perceived by some as a role and if someone is not gifted or does not particularly enjoy it, they disengage expecting others to assume responsibility. The nature of officership is we all find ourselves embracing roles we may not naturally be gifted at. I am no different to any other officer and there have been aspects of ministry I haven't necessarily enjoyed, yet in serving it is surprising how God often works and there is a deep joy that follows.

I am certainly not suggesting it is compulsory corps officers do all the caring - that would be quite ridiculous - yet they do need to demonstrate leadership by ensuring it takes place. At the risk of being too confronting, many small corps have less people connected than were in the songsters (choir) at Perth Fortress in our time and we managed 400+ connected people with empowered soldiers ministering alongside us.

People are our business and 'heaven on earth' is what we want them to experience now as well as life eternal. Ensuring an effective framework exists to care for people is helped by the Senior Pastoral Care Council (once known as Senior Census Locals) with corps officers and key spiritually mature soldiers driving this ministry. At its best, this can see tremendous outcomes in discipling and caring for people, embodying the philosophy that 'rolls mean souls' as often quoted to me by Debra.

I have often sensed a lack of clarity about the purpose and practice of this key leadership group. Whilst some corps understandably consider the Corps Council or Corps Leadership Team to be the most important group, the Senior Pastoral Care Council has a higher purpose and demands a higher standard of commitment by those serving on it. The appointment of soldiers to this body demands they have a high level of spiritual maturity, good interpersonal skills, preparedness to sacrificially serve and be examples of true Salvationism.

Meetings of this group are not merely about reconciling rolls for statistical purposes, the focus is about the spiritual wellbeing of those in our sphere of influence. This is a spiritual ministry involving an administrative function; how a corps officer leads this group will dictate the culture and shape the outcomes achieved.

When people have a passion burning within to care holistically for others, God will honour that and the work of the Holy Spirit will become evident to all.

One practical suggestion I often share is about the importance of first visits when you meet someone. As officers change corps appointments or people transfer to a new congregation, you get a fantastic opportunity to ask the most basic questions without apology. You can very easily gauge the depth of someone's faith by the way they respond to foundational questions about their faith journey and current relationship with Christ. Make the most of the opportunity those first visits present, which will not as readily be available in subsequent visits where people are sometimes guarded about openly sharing.

I would also meet with people wanting to transfer to Perth Fortress Corps, eager to ensure they understood our values. Part of my objective was to also ensure any unresolved conflict was dealt with appropriately. Similarly, when someone chose to transfer from our corps, our desire was to ensure there were no outstanding concerns; we wished to send them with the blessing of our corps.

I trust you are getting the message that as corps officers, Debra and I gave pastoral visitation a high priority. Debra in particular often invested up to several days every week in proactive caring, whilst I by necessity adopted a more reactive approach based on what was happening in the life of the corps.

Perth Fortress grew quite significantly in our time at the corps and God was certainly at work. Finding how we could see everyone connected and cared for was becoming a nice problem to have. Debra was particularly concerned about this and we had learnt the best way for people to feel connected and cared for was to have people serving or part of a group. This resonated with our leaders and it wasn't long before the catchphrase became 'every group a praying group; every group a caring group'. We also embraced the priority of all people connected with the corps being encouraged to engage in some form of actual ministry.

What needs to be very clear is we were still accountable and accepted responsibility for the caring and discipling ministries of the corps. The reality is people will fall between the cracks, so we would meet every week with several leaders and carers to review what was happening in people's lives. It was from this framework we identified those needing to be followed up and we were indebted to a corps member who maintained a weekly attendance list (this was a massive exercise).

Imagine my surprise when sharing with some younger officers, I have sensed confusion from them about what they should actually do on a visit. Whilst there were times when it was logical to make an appointment to see someone, we were often dropping by unannounced to see people.

A typical visit doesn't require you to spend 3 hours with someone as if you were there as their friend (albeit that can become the case). The best visits were often only 30 - 45 minutes with a very intentional approach to raising faith questions and sharing prayer. Lunchtime catch ups or having coffee together can work really well provided you go with a mindset to ask the right questions and not just socialise. Ultimately, this is about relationships and developing a level of trust that allows us to speak into the life of that person we seek to care for.

I am really pleased to sense many corps becoming more astute in their welcoming practices at worship. It seems so basic, yet it really makes a difference when people are greeted well to worship. The flip side is it can feel awkward and downright uncomfortable when this is done poorly. I recently had an experience when visiting a corps on holidays and feeling I wasn't valued; it was much more interesting for the welcomers to spend time with their uniformed friends. I wonder who needed the welcome more and why was I treated differently after worship when someone realised who I was?

This area became a focus for us at Perth Fortress, so we resolved to provide some basic training to help the team. We wanted them to understand what the objective was and then have a framework that would guide how they greeted people. Fortunately we had a couple open to work with us on this in Harvey and Gloria Reynolds. I was trying to explain the basics of the importance of a great hello, whilst looking people in the eye and giving them your full attention. They needed to feel valued and we also needed to be alert to how we could assimilate them into our fellowship.

We had prepared the key leaders of ministry groups and a range of people so we could 'link' first time visitors with someone straight away. As we all know, people are looking for a relational connection when they are exploring new churches often more than they are the worship experience or preaching (not that these things are unimportant).

To help the team have a framework to work from, I coined a phrase that Harvey and Gloria wouldn't forget. I told Harvey he should think about his wife's lips that he loved to kiss (that got his attention I recall). He needed to remember "**G**loria's **L**uscious **L**ips" or 'GLL' which stood for 3 key things. The framework was to '**G**reet' with an extended hand and smile with a positive word of welcome, whilst 'Looking' them in the eye and not being distracted by other people. The final challenge was to immediately try and 'Link' a first time visitor either with a person who led a ministry that might suit them or someone who could sit with them. Many corps and churches have far more sophisticated systems in place, yet "GLL" was right for us at that time.

The key message to remember is that everyone plays a role in pastoral ministry and assimilation, yet ultimate responsibility rests with the corps officers. For Debra and me, pastoral ministry was an important priority.

A moment of obvious joy as we led together in a divisional meeting during our time in the Western Victoria Division.

Platform Ministry

THERE ARE AMPLE RESOURCES AND far more qualified people to speak into the issue of worship leadership and preaching than me. I find leading worship and preaching a joy and have been affirmed over the years about my approach and engagement with people. Given there are not a great deal of Salvationist writers making comment on this area, I offer my own high level views to stimulate your thinking.

As a corps officer, I would spend each Wednesday preparing my message and meeting lead. For all of my officership, we had 2 or 3 meetings each Sunday and that meant I always found myself needing to prepare 2 messages per week when preaching. In our early officership, I did the majority of preaching and planning for worship. The season of life we were in with young children saw Debra preferring to have me take on these responsibilities and she would preach only occasionally. She would still lead part of worship every week and commenced preaching more regularly in our latter years of corps officership.

In my time at Warrnambool and Perth Fortress, I would invest heavily in my morning message and often do something different in the evening. Most officers find themselves only preaching one message per week these days. Believe it or not, there was a time at Kaniva when we had 4 meetings one week each month requiring 3 separate messages.

To be honest, I wouldn't say I preached overly well on a consistent basis during my time at Kaniva. There were too many times when I felt dissatisfied as I stood to share God's message. Managing a large workload whilst we had young children and covering multiple locations was not easy, plus I was still on a steep learning curve in the various day to day aspects of officership.

Once we moved to Warrnambool, I found that being able to dedicate more time to preparation plus benefiting from experience quickly enhanced my preaching. Similarly, I discovered a new freedom in leading worship and realised how much I enjoyed it, albeit I often found myself playing in the brass band or bass guitar. To this day, I relish the opportunity to preach and lead worship.

I worked hard to choose the best songs to thematically fit the theme for worship. When using the contemporary group (for want of a better title) I would pay attention to the key and how the music would flow. What a blessing it is to have good musical support and this enhances the flow of worship immensely. To have scope to pray, read scripture and speak over inspired music is incredibly powerful and I find really helps people be drawn into the presence of God. As a musician, I would promise the piano player to never leave them high and dry when they were 'vamping' to help enrich the worship time. If you have a musical background, it is worth working with your pianist/keyboard player to develop an understanding, including the signals you will use to help communicate what you plan on doing next.

One of the advantages of having broad musical capability was I saw ways to use varying styles and forms of music in worship. This became particularly helpful at Perth Fortress where it was quite a challenge to move from a very traditional musical repertoire to a more diverse and varied approach. What worked was insisting on the contemporary group using arrangements of traditional songs and requiring the band and songsters to broaden their repertoire to ensure we were often using kit drum to change the feel. Towards the latter part of my time at Perth Fortress, I also chose to select what would be played for the offering to ensure alignment with the theme and desired style of music. There were good outcomes from this overall strategic approach and I was quite well supported by several key people.

One of my pet hates in worship is where there are significant gaps without purpose; I cringe when the experience of connecting with God is hampered because of poor planning. To be fair to those who may struggle musically and with this general concept, I accept it can be a challenge to understand and implement if it hasn't been well modelled. I would like to think those who served with me over the years would understand how I approached this and the difference it can make.

Back to the matter of preaching; why is it that so many people read their entire sermon? I accept it is not for everyone to preach without notes and remain focused on the key themes of their message, yet most people can surely share a personal story without being totally reliant on notes. When I worked with cadets, all of them were able to do this at a minimum because we would regularly work at it together.

I was with Captains Peter and Erica Jones recently who spent quite some time under my leadership as Candidate Helpers at the Hamilton Hill Corps in Western Australia. Erica shared her memories of 'preaching' to me on a Friday afternoon in preparation for Sunday and having both myself and Peter provide ongoing critiquing throughout. She is now a fine speaker and has continued to be open to learn how best to prepare and communicate. Like so many aspects of officership, we owe it to God to apply ourselves to achieving our full potential.

My own personal journey to develop confidence and not be totally reliant on notes started in my car. I would pick a random topic and simply talk out loud (when I was driving alone you'll be pleased to know) and this helped me greatly. When I preach without notes, I tend to rely on either multimedia or specific words in the scripture reading to be memory prompts for me. I truly believe there are many officers who could significantly improve their preaching if they would only apply themselves. I am pleased about the recent initiative to run a Preaching Bootcamp in the Australia Southern Territory each year to provide development opportunities in this ministry area.

Communication methods will continue to evolve in sharing the gospel, with ever increasing high quality media resources available to aide this ministry. My own style has always preferred preaching to have a strong scripture base driving my message, rather than adopting a more topical approach. Preachers will obviously develop their own style which is to be encouraged, provided the truth of the gospel is presented without compromise. Ultimately, the message needs to impact on people's daily lives and there always need to be clarity about the foundational message of salvation when that is the key theme.

Two key questions I ask myself when preparing my messages are 'how' and 'so what'. When speaking about what our faith requires of us, we need to share practical ways for people to actually implement the key message. That means if we are highlighting the importance of being people of integrity, we need to help them understand how they can do that in practical terms. It is not enough to merely tell them what they should be doing, or worse still highlight what they are not doing.

We also need to recognise some people will listen and deep down be thinking 'so what'. Consumerism is increasingly impacting Australian culture and people are often sceptical, wondering how they will benefit from all manner of things. Great preachers will effectively communicate with passion and clearly address the 'so what' question with compelling logic and inspiring hope, as well as providing clarity about how to apply biblical teaching in everyday situations.

In our changing society, people continue to willingly sit and listen to a preacher in a wide range of worship settings. How long people actively listen - and indeed how long this remains culturally our practice - may well depend on how effectively the message is being delivered. Even I drift off when listening to boring or poorly prepared speakers, so why should we expect anything different from others.

Whilst not everyone is gifted in this area, those who have untapped potential owe it to those listening to them – and to God – to invest themselves in being the very best they can be.

But how can they call on him to save them unless they believe in him? And how can they believe in him if they have never heard about him? And how can they hear about him unless someone tells them? And how will anyone go and tell them without being sent? That is why the Scriptures say, "How beautiful are the feet of messengers who bring good news!"
Romans 10:14, 15 (NLT)

When People Criticise

OFFICERSHIP BY ITS VERY NATURE is both an enormous privilege and immense challenge at the same time. The demands can be incredibly draining, whilst also breathing energy and life into us. Only by being secure in who we are as people, called and equipped by God, can we ever hope to flourish as spiritual leaders.

There will be difficult times in the midst of everyday ministry and this is the lot of all leaders. It may seem to be one of the current buzz words, yet I can't stress enough how important it is to have high EQ (often referred to as emotional quotient or emotional intelligence). This can be a natural attribute for some people, yet I firmly believe it can be developed if you are teachable and regularly reflect on leadership experiences. Learning how to cope with criticism and people who are downright rude will help you survive and lead through difficulties.

There have been times when I have managed situations poorly and too quickly 'shot a response from the hip' when I should have been more circumspect. It is a skill to generically respond to criticism or verbal attacks and generate precious seconds to be more considered in words of response. This is a skill that can be learnt if you commit yourself to it. For me, taking a few seconds allows me to respond from a leadership perspective or calmly delay further dialogue to a more appropriate time rather than responding emotionally.

I see many leaders getting unduly angry and responding emotionally when the issues are actually petty and on occasions simply require strong leadership to come to the fore. An officer who doesn't believe these skills can be developed has likely never actually opened themselves up to role playing predictable situations. People will make angry critical comment about predictable matters, so it is logical to develop a leadership framework from which you can respond to them.

The importance of good listening should never be underestimated and learning to ask great questions can assist in disarming difficult situations. Many books and seminars are available on this subject and most leaders are exposed to such teaching. The key is to put it into practice and I often find myself using phrases such as "help me understand …" and "what would it look like …"

When things become heated, my experience is I manage best when I discipline myself to control my breathing and remain silent for a few precious seconds. This can provide enough of a buffer to allow you a greater level of control in how you then choose to respond.

Over the years I have learnt a great deal by observing how other leaders use phrases which gently push back and redirect conversations. You don't need to allow the tone and message from a critic to dictate your response to them. You can often disarm a potentially emotionally charged discussion simply by responding in an open and gracious manner that acknowledges their feelings and frustrations. I encourage you to try this and reflect on personal experiences to discover how you can do this better.

Whatever your situation, it doesn't take great imagination to envisage those situations where people will potentially criticise you at some stage. Don't hesitate to indicate you are happy to give their thoughts considered reflection, after which you can speak further with them. Whatever it may be for you, find a strategy that allows you to speak words of calm in the midst of what could become an unnecessarily fiery and unhelpful discussion.

Well-developed conflict resolution skills are essential to survive the predictable critical feedback that will come. Whilst the foundational skills can be learnt in seminars and workshops, only when you find yourself managing live situations will you refine these skills. Don't be too hard on yourself and expect too much too quickly; it will take some time and experience to have a clear framework to operate from. Regrettably, there will be ample learning opportunities with the prevalence of people now using email to instantly share their concerns.

I received a rather critical letter from a soldier on one occasion, making some very blunt sweeping statements about a significant issue. Although I felt my response was appropriately gracious, I effectively sought to justify my position and provide additional context to the issue in a defensive manner. This was far from a wise strategy to manage conflict when having a coffee together would almost certainly have been more productive.

Sometime later, I found myself reflecting on the real issue at the heart of this situation. In the midst of everything, there was the proverbial 'kernel of truth' I needed to hear and take action on. The leadership approach of the corps (which I was responsible for as leader) was to carefully manage how much information would be openly shared with the corps. Not surprisingly, this left a void of information that people chose to fill in their own way.

Whilst the key message of that letter may have been ill-informed, the lack of transparent information being shared could not be ignored. I needed to acknowledge that better communication needed to take place if I expected people to commit wholeheartedly to the journey.

What transpired was a renewed focus and commitment to communicating widely with the corps through multiple methods. This was extremely well received and had very positive impact especially on the morale of older members of the corps. Increasing morale may not sound like a very spiritual outcome, yet when people have a positive mindset it manifests missionally as they invest in the life of the corps.

From that time, we resolved to be as transparent about issues as we possibly could, other than when to do so would hinder the mission or potentially be harmful to someone.

Criticism will definitely come, so don't be surprised when it happens. As one local officer would often say to me, "Bruce, you're not paid to be popular!"

> If you listen to constructive criticism,
> you will be at home among the wise.
> *Proverbs 15:31 (NLT)*

Corps Management

WHATEVER THE ROLE OR EMPLOYMENT someone has, there is almost always some degree of administration required. It is simply a fact that any situation involving business practices demands that a level of governance and accountability be observed. Here are some general principles that have shaped my practices throughout my officership.

I work more effectively when I have an orderly workspace without undue distractions. Paying attention to aesthetics pays significant dividends in the outcomes I achieve.

It is wise to allocate specific time for administration in your schedule and resist the temptation to multitask too much with social media and other matters. I sense many people operate extremely inefficiently because they try to juggle too many functions at once.

You need a system to manage incoming and outgoing paper based correspondence, i.e. letters, invoices, statements, governance related documents, etc. If you are unsure how to best structure this, ask for guidance from your leaders who will offer recommendations.

In some appointments, I have progressively developed template letters to use for recurring matters needing to be dealt with. This will ultimately save you time and also assist in maintaining a consistent standard of presentation.

Manage your email appropriately so it doesn't end up managing you. Don't open emails without having a strategy about how you then deal with them. A big trap is opening them on a mobile device and leaving them as 'read' meaning you need to remember to deal with them. I always mark them 'unread' if I need to take action at a later time.

It is important to return your phone calls and almost always on the day you receive them, yet acknowledging there are occasional instances where it is prudent to delay a response for a day or two. I notice when people repetitively fail to return calls or answer correspondence.

Meet deadlines or if it is impossible to do so, be courteous enough to communicate you will be late and when you will meet the required expectation. You need to accept there will be occasions where failing to meet a deadline will not be well received, especially on priority matters where ample forward notice has been provided.

A wise leader will empower local officers to undertake administrative duties within their area of ministry and ensure they have clarity about what authority they have. Resist the temptation to micromanage them, yet ensure you do hold them accountable for agreed outcomes. Remember also to find ways to consistently acknowledge what they are doing and thank them.

Whilst it is expected you will always follow policy, be aware the standard is unapologetically high when it involves the safety of others. A good example is the Australia Southern Territory's stringent framework of integrity checking and training for everyone working with vulnerable people. This is a high priority matter where your own leadership needs to reinforce policy, taking decisive action when it is not complied with. In such cases, the safety of those we minister to demands our personal attention.

As hard as it might be to hear, just do it! You'll be surprised what you can get done in the time some people spend complaining or procrastinating about administration.

There is also a range of simple principles that you will be wise to observe when it comes to property matters. It frustrates me when large planned maintenance balances accrue whilst buildings deteriorate and unnecessary damage is the result. This is simply poor stewardship; small problems become major ones when left unresolved over an extended timeframe.

Rather than have routine property matters clog up leadership team meetings, I instigated a Property Committee at both Warrnambool and Perth Fortress. In both situations, these were not groups that met for hours on end and discussed things; these were action oriented groups. With the support of key leadership, we gave the committee a defined level of authority where they could take action on issues. Only when the work was to cost more than their approved budget or encroach on a known sensitive matter would the broader leadership group be involved. The best outcome of this was to free up our leadership team meetings with time to address more significant mission matters and invest in teaching.

I have special memories of working to have the outside toilets at Broughton replaced in my final year. I smile as I think of my daughter, Kerry, who would insist we visited one of the local farms on the way home from meetings if 'nature' was calling.

The corps was unable to fund this project, yet the division generously supported us to undertake a basic upgrade, including inside toilet facilities. The lesson here is that when dealing with property matters and there are no available funds locally, the responsible thing is to ensure divisional leadership are aware of the need. That way a broader consideration of the relative priority can be made in the context of the whole division and available resources. It also ensures there is clarity about the condition of properties when officers change.

Good corps management requires us to ensure appropriate systems and practices are in place so we can consistently be good stewards of all that God has entrusted us with.

Following the successful refurbishment of the Kaniva Hall, my next challenge was to upgrade the toilets at Broughton to indoor ones.

Measuring Success

THIS HAS BEEN A RATHER topical issue in recent times and I will simply share my overarching perspective; you measure what you value.

My views will not be shared by all, yet most people agree it can be a challenge to make an informed assessment about when people have come into a relationship with Christ.

Don't complain to me about being unsure how to record it in SAMIS (the statistical recording tool for the Australia Southern Territory). If this is the key objective of our International Army, then surely we will find the answer to how to record it. It is always cause for celebration when someone comes to know Christ personally and we would add their name to the Recruits Roll. This became a helpful reference point when considering who should be targeted for discipleship purposes and eventually soldiership.

A related observation I would make is motivated self-led officers ask questions and find solutions to an incredibly broad range of matters. On the other hand, there are those who focus on perceived complexity and blame systems for not being easy to use. Leaders find a way in the midst of messiness and aren't afraid to ask questions and provide suggested solutions when they notice a problem needing a response.

The setting of goals is part of our leadership culture and you need to quickly come to grips with how to approach this. It is not surprising there are a wide range of perspectives on how goals are best set and what produces the best outcomes.

Personally, I found it helpful to have clear measurable goals that didn't require some interpretative 'touchy feely' analysis to indicate if it had been met or not. As mentioned earlier, I'm attracted to strategies that produce the culture required for the outcomes I want to see achieved. I'm not suggesting these should be either/or, rather when goals promote healthy culture the missional outcomes will likely follow.

In reality, the development of a healthy culture becomes part of the strategy to achieve the stated goals. In my case, the first 4 years at Perth Fortress were quite a struggle at times, yet as the culture progressively changed we began to see the outcomes emerge quite naturally. This was really exciting and noticeable in ways that would often surprise us.

I believe it is appropriate to embrace both approaches to goal setting with measures in place so you can hold yourself accountable.

Being Faithful

SCRIPTURE TELLS US WE WILL give account for our life's investment, knowing that Jesus will be our advocate and present us to the Father. The blessing of being a child of God is an exceptional gift to be cherished and warrants our full dedication to Him.

Whether we are called to serve Him as activist soldiers in a local Salvation Army Corps, officers in a worldwide Army or committed servants in a local church community, God deserves and demands our best. The encouragement I give to my children and my fellow Christians is simply this; be the best you can possibly be - that's all that God asks of you.

When there is so much that can demand our attention, it is helpful to remind ourselves of what ultimately matters most in Christian ministry. The words of Jesus are a poignant reminder of where we should focus our efforts when he said:

> 'Love the Lord your God with all your heart and with all your soul and with all your mind.' This is the first and greatest commandment. And the second is like it: 'Love your neighbour as yourself.'
>
> Matthew 22:37-39 (NIV)

Always remember;

Honour God and He will honour you!

Family has a way of keeping you grounded; what a joy it is when one of my grandsons pays me a visit. Here I am with Malachi who dropped in to see grandad at Territorial Headquarters.

About the Author

Lieut. Colonel Bruce Stevens is strongly passionate about the Kingdom of God and particularly energised by opportunities to develop effective leaders.

Prior to officership, Bruce worked as a Corporate Tax Consultant and those business skills have proven to be a great asset in his subsequent ministry. Bruce holds a Bachelor of Business (Accounting) and was accepted as a Certified Practising Accountant in 1985.

Commissioned as an officer in 1992, he previously served in corps and divisional headquarters appointments. His first eight years were in the Western Victoria Division, having spent four years at Kaniva/Broughton Corps and then moving to Warrnambool Corps for a further four years. An eight year appointment at Perth Fortress Corps in Western Australia followed.

A one year additional appointment as Corps Programme Consultant preceded a three year appointment as Divisional Secretary in Western Australia. During this time Bruce had extensive responsibilities for finance, property, general business matters, as well as providing leadership support as second in command.

Together with his wife Debra, he recently led the Western Victoria Division for three years as Divisional Commander. Bruce brings a broad range of experience to his current role as Secretary for Business Administration in the Australia Southern Territory. He also provides leadership as the Executive Officer of the Melbourne Staff Band, a role he is greatly fulfilled in and which provides many ministry opportunities.

Married for 35 years to Debra, they have 2 children. Kerry is married to Glenn Smith and they are officers serving in a corps. Mitchell is married to Sally and they are Auxiliary-Lieutenants, also serving at a corps. Bruce and Debra are blessed with 4 grandsons, being a source of great joy for them.

Bruce enjoys a wide range of sports, relishes the opportunity to use his musical abilities and continues to have an active interest in the finance industry.

24469617R00057

Printed in Great Britain
by Amazon